MRO
PURCHASING

Peter L. Grieco, Jr.

PT Publications, Inc.
P.O. Box 310266
Miami, FL 33231

Library of Congress Cataloging in Publication Data

Grieco, Peter L., 1942-
    MRO purchasing / Peter L. Grieco, Jr.
        p. cm.
    Includes index.
    ISBN 0-945456-44-1
    1. Industrial procurement--Management. 2. Materials
    management.
  I.   Title
    HD39.5.G747   1996
    658.7'2--dc20   96-30412
                                                 CIP

Table of Contents

ABOUT THE AUTHOR: Peter L. Grieco, Jr., is President and Chief Executive Officer of Professionals for Technology Associates, Inc., an international consulting and education firm specializing in the areas of Just-In-Time, Total Quality Control, Automation and Systems Implementation. He was active in the development of Apple Computer's Macintosh Automated Focus Factory in Fremont, California. His industry experience encompasses both repetitive and discrete manufacturing processes. He has more than twenty-five years of experience as a practitioner and educator in the manufacturing environment. He has held numerous operation and financial positions.

Mr. Grieco presently serves on the Stanford Research Institute Advisory Board (SRI) and is a member of the American Society for Quality Control (ASQC), the National Association of Purchasing Management, and the American Production and Inventory Control Society (APICS) where he has held positions as: Education and Research Foundation Director, National Secretary/Treasurer, Vice President of Region I (New England), and Past President of the Hartford chapter.

Mr. Grieco is the coauthor of the latest JIT/TQC textbooks, "Made In America - The Total Business Concept," "Just-In-Time Purchasing," "Supplier Certification," "Behind Bars: Bar Coding Principles and Applications," "The World of Negotiations: Never Being A Loser," and "World Class: Measuring Its Achievements." He attended Central Connecticut State University and Wharton School of Finance (Moody's School of Commerce). He is a frequent lecturer for numerous professional societies, seminars, conferences, and numerous university programs on Operations Management and Just-In-Time/Total Quality Control related topics. He is also recognized in Inventory Management for his contribution to education and training.

INTRODUCTION

CHAPTER ONE

What is MRO?

MRO procurement, or the purchasing of material, repairs and operating supplies, is an overlooked area of business which is rich with potential savings. It is incorrect to think that office supplies, the services of heating or air conditioning technicians or temporary help in the mailroom don't have a significant impact on the cost of running a business, manufacturing a product or providing a service. MRO procurement has a large monetary impact on your business. For that reason alone, their procurement should not be delegated solely to the lowest level personnel in the purchasing department.

Some say that 25-30% of all manufacturing, maintenance and operating parts can be accounted for by MRO consumables. Other procurement experts contend that the process of purchasing and managing these items can account for as much as 75% of a company's supply chain resources. This can translate into a financial impact of between $.35 to $.50 out of each dollar used to purchase these MRO items.

Let us provide you with an example to consider. If you were to compare the amount of money in signed checks from the Accounts Payable function to the money expended by signed purchase orders, you would discover a very surprising fact. Between 40 to 50% of the issued checks *do not* go through the purchasing department. They represent purchases made by non-purchasing professionals who are not skilled in negotiation and purchasing techniques. Certainly, this is an area to address when reigning in MRO procurement.

It's clear that there are opportunities for the purchasing function to save money and resources if they attack MRO procurement in the same systematic manner that ticket items of greater value have been approached. In short, this entails a combination of supplier certification for distributors and service providers, inventory management, total costing and sophisticated buying/planning techniques. The benefits that will be gained from this type of campaign are considerable as the list below demonstrates:

- **More complete control of purchasing.**
- **Reduction of total operating costs.**
- **Continued pricing consistency.**
- **Reduction of paperwork errors.**
- **Improved allocation of scarce resources.**
- **Dramatic purchasing cost reductions.**
- **Modernized inventory management.**
- **Standardization of procedures.**

And the most valued benefit is this: Bringing MRO purchases under control enables you to focus on continuous improvement and consolidation of the supply base, both of which will yield substantial cost reductions.

Define five MRO objectives you would like to achieve and how they will improve your buying performance.

1 _____

2 _____

3 _____

4 _____

5 _____

New Strategies for MRO Procurement

What we are saying in this book is that the attention usually placed on direct purchases should now *also* be placed on indirect purchases. Although tactics differ for each kind of purchase, many of the strategies are similar. The predominant strategy for MRO procurement is consolidation of suppliers, or reduction of the supply base. There are a number of ways to achieve this end.

Consolidation of suppliers

Commodity management. Commodity management is a team effort at reducing the supply base, consolidating pricing, reducing cost and guaranteeing quality levels and delivery schedules which meet a company's requirements.

Material positioning. Pro-Tech's Material Positioning tool can help your company choose an effective supply strategy for each MRO commodity and supplier. The tool is based upon the recognition that two of the most important factors which determine supply strategy are: 1) influence on company results and 2) procurement risks. In order to understand how these factors influence your company, you need to assess each of your MRO suppliers, even though most will be noncritical in nature, according to the following steps:

- **Determine influences on company results.**
    - **Determine market success elements.**
    - **Weight elements relative to market success.**
    - **Calculate index of influence on company result.**

- **Calculate procurement risk.**
    - **Determine relative strength of competitive forces.**
        - **Bargaining power.**
        - **Rivalry.**
        - **Substitution.**
        - **Entry barriers.**
    - **Position material on matrix.**

- **Select appropriate strategy.**

The quadrant the supplier/commodity occupies in the Material Positioning Matrix shown in Figure 1-1 will assist you in determining the most appropriate strategies for MRO procurement.

When used properly, the matrix positions the selected supplier/commodity in a specific box that requires you to develop and refine a strategy for this specific commodity. Figure 1-2 shows some of the dominant strategies that can be used in MRO supply management.

When selecting your supply strategy, be aware that the position on the matrix and the strength of the indices influences strategy selection. Note also that your overall process may include multiple strategies or require you to shift suppliers based on new information. Clients who have used these tools find that they are much better able to effectively assess their MRO supply base.

Supplier selection. The actual criteria you choose to select MRO suppliers will vary according to the size and nature of your business. Each company will have to tailor and develop its own checklist. However, there are criteria which are common to every industry and the process of development itself is extremely important since it is an exercise in creating an integrated approach within your company. Our

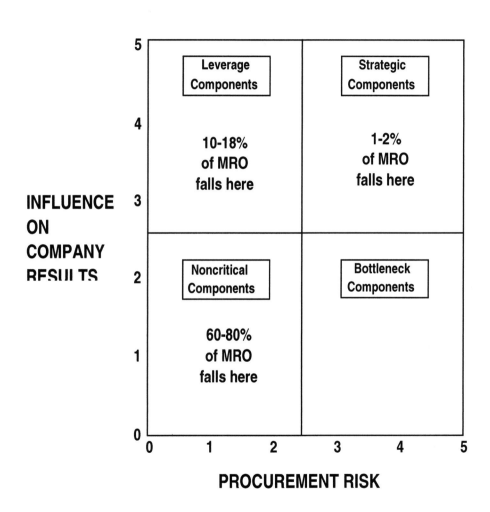

Figure 1-1.

PROCUREMENT STRATEGIES

	Strategic	Leverage	Bottleneck	Noncritical
Blanket Orders	X	X		X
Standardization	X	X	X	X
Quality Improvement	X	X		
Cost Reduction	X	X		X
Consolidate with other Suppliers		X		X
Supplier Stocking	X	X		X
Competitive Bidding		X		X
Price Rollback		X		X
Supplier Reduction		X		X

DEFINITIONS

BLANKET ORDERS — Negotiate longer term agreement to reduce/ stabilize pricing, cost, delivery and/or improve quality.

STANDARDIZATION — Design changes to allow for use of industry standard and/or reduce product proliferation.

QUALITY IMPROVEMENT — Improve quality through process mapping, process control, capability study, etc.

COST REDUCTION — Reduce cost of doing business by Kanban, EDI, blanket orders, etc.

CONSOLIDATE WITH OTHER SUPPLIERS — Negotiate on consolidated volumes of other suppliers.

SUPPLIER STOCKING — Negotiate with supplier to deliver to point of use.

COMPETITIVE BIDDING — Negotiate with two or more suppliers.

PRICE ROLLBACK — Ask existing supplier to match price of competitive source.

SUPPLIER REDUCTION — Reduce the number of suppliers for a commodity in order to increase leverage and reduce cost of doing business.

Figure 1-2.

Supplier Certification Video Education Series illustrates how companies can develop their own MRO supplier selection criteria using this approach. With this in mind, let's look in more detail at some of the criteria you will want to consider. The following list is in no particular order of importance:

MRO SUPPLIER SELECTION CRITERIA

Source of Supply	Capability
Financial Condition	Inventory Levels
Geographical Location	Capacity and Flexibility
Quality History	Facilities and Equipment
Customer Base	Labor Conditions
Education and Training	Cost Control
Quality Management	Knowledgeable Sales Force
Competitive Pricing	On-time Delivery
Organization and Staffing	Policies and Procedures
Subsupplier Management	Housekeeping
Ethics	Quantity
Performance	EDI Capability
Point of Manufacturing	Bar Coding Capability
Breadth of Product Offering	Stocking Programs
Environmental Programs	National Presences
(Reusables)	

Although there are many categories listed above, most companies typically look at less than 50% of them when they select an MRO supplier. Traditionally, they give an order based on price when issuing purchase orders to a new supplier. In fact, MRO buyers in many companies are still measured by the number of POs they place per week.

Once you have drawn up a list of criteria, your next step is to consolidate the categories so there is no duplication and then prepare a Request for Proposal. Assigning a point value to each category can help you determine where to draw the line for those MRO suppliers who qualify. The qualifying score can vary, but the higher, the better.

In the past, companies have selected MRO suppliers haphazardly. A goal of developing supplier selection criteria is to shrink the supply base. Achieving this goal depends upon how many suppliers we need for each MRO service, product and commodity. It may be that we need two suppliers for office supplies and two for HVAC (heating, ventilation and air conditioning) services when we start the program. We may be able to lower this figure as the program gets underway. We don't want to move too quickly, however. We don't want to set a goal of going from 500 suppliers to 100 if that endangers our comfort level.

Certification programs. The ultimate goal of Supplier Certification is to develop a mutually beneficial partnership between your company and your MRO suppliers. While only strategic suppliers go through full certification, the certification process or parts of it apply to all suppliers. Chapter Seven of *Supplier Certification II: A Handbook for Achieving Excellence Through Continuous Improvement* (PT Publications) and Chapter Thirteen of the *Supply Management Toolbox* (PT Publications) provide several excellent examples of the tools of certification: partnership agreements, long-term supply contracts, confidentiality agreements, and much more useful information. In this section, we want to provide you with an overview of the phases of MRO Supplier Certification and how they fit into the model of the entire Supply Management process. (See Figure 1-3.)

The purpose of Phase One is to work with MRO suppliers who can qualify to be in the program on the basis of the MRO supplier survey. Remember that many of the suppliers you survey may never obtain certification in the first two years of your effort. However, improvements occur throughout the process, not just upon qualifying as a certified supplier. The first step in determining whether a supplier can become a partner is to assess the present state of its business and its commodity range.

PHASES OF
SUPPLIER CERTIFICATION

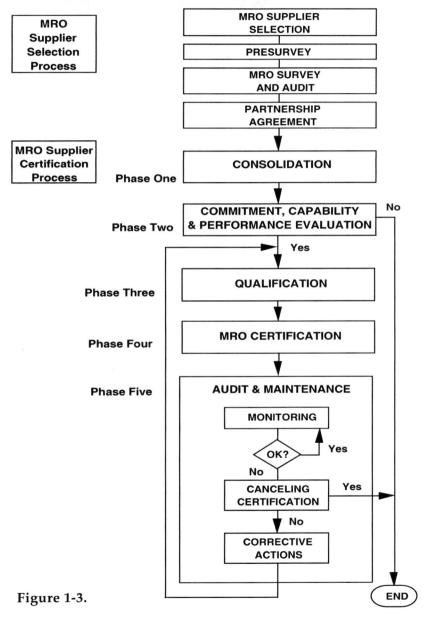

Figure 1-3.

Phase Two takes the information generated in the first phase and subjects it to an intense analysis in your first efforts to reduce the supply base. The goal of this program review and evaluation is to decide whether an MRO supplier is ready to proceed and what it is required to do in order to improve before any more progress can be made.

In Phase Three, the buyer takes the steps necessary to set up an initial evaluation of the MRO supplier's ability to meet delivery, quantity and quality requirements. Phase Four is the actual certification stage in which the supplier proves it can perform to requirements. The fifth and final phase of the certification process cannot be overlooked. In many ways, it is the most important since it defines the process of auditing and maintaining the supplier's control over its processes. This phase may entail going through a corrective action loop to assure that the supplier can match the exacting customer demands for the commodity.

Surveys and audits. In general, the criteria in a survey or audit of an MRO supplier looks for the presence of sound total business conditions which are under control. This forms the basis for surveys of MRO suppliers.

A survey is used to select capable MRO suppliers. An audit of MRO suppliers can be thought of as a calibration tool, whereby you can check to see that the supplier's quality and performance remain under control. Since the value of MRO supplies is relatively low, companies spend very little time trying to improve a supplier's performance. Instead, companies simply move on to the next supplier. But, if more time was spent on educating and training, this ultimately self-defeating activity would not be necessary. For those who need assistance in establishing your own surveys and audits, we recommend that you view Tape #4 in our Video Education Series, *Supplier Certification: The Path to Excellence.*

In evaluating your MRO suppliers, all surveys and audits must employ quantifiable questions. Fuzzy questions only elicit fuzzy answers. The answers to your surveys and audits must be objectively quantified. In Chapter Three, we provide an example of a supplier survey and an evaluation scale to use when rating MRO suppliers.

Utilization of Distributors

Many companies utilize distributors when purchasing their MRO supplies. Controlling costs is difficult with this type of supplier. If you are a high volume buyer, you can exert control over the requirements which the distributor puts on each of its sub-tier suppliers. If you aren't a high volume buyer, then you should make every effort to find distributors who have a rigorous internal selection process in place and who maintain an excellent quality profile for the companies they represent. Future Electronics, a Massachusetts firm, has started a World Class program for distribution in which their customers can do one-stop shopping. The company's objective is to negotiate a win/win arrangement with suppliers so that their customers can purchase 100 percent of their electronic components from Future. In exchange, Future will supply kits of material as required (Just-In-Time) and help customers avoid stocking inventory.

Distribution and warehousing are often overlooked in the world class arena. We hear so much about world class manufacturing that we have begun to believe that JIT, TQM and other world class techniques are only for manufacturing folks. This couldn't be further from the truth. Every area of a company needs to address cycle time reduction and the elimination of waste. This is because the trend of the future is to ship all products from each manufacturing site directly to the point of use. Obviously, distribution and warehousing will play an even more significant role in this future. The key is to work together when addressing these issues.

One of our clients in the office supplies industry worked with a distributor to reduce 400 purchase orders and 450 invoices per month to one blanket agreement which requires only 12 invoices per year, or one per month. With the average cost to a issue a single PO at $125, the savings were $60,000 in addition to the savings on invoices. The company was even able to redeploy one accounts payable person after implementing this action and spreading it to other commodities.

Companies need to address the concerns needed to assess the function of distribution. In our *Supply Management Toolbox* (PT Publications), we provide a complete MRO Supplier Survey and Audit. The list below includes all of the important issues, but it is not intended to be complete. Each company, depending on the complexity of their distribution function, will add elements it deems necessary.

1.   Does the distributor's policies and procedures identify customer on-time demands and requirements?

2.   What level of commitment does the distributor attain in customer service?

3.   What methods of inventory control are used to balance multiple stocking locations both within the center and the network? Does the distributor understand customer supply chain issues?

4.   Will they provide RMA numbers for any returns?

5.   What modes of distribution are used and how are they chosen? Do they have national and pan-European service?

6.   How are distribution routes selected and managed for frequent deliveries? Large or small lots?

7.   How does the distributor determine your requirements?

8.   Does the distributor utilize EDI and on-line inventory management?

9.   Will the distributor provide a team to assess your requirements?

10. **How will the distributor eliminate customer back orders in order to achieve 100% customer satisfaction?**

11. **Will the distributor consolidate your requirements for other items?**

Other MRO Procurement Strategies

One MRO procurement strategy which will require some careful attention is whether to buy goods and services from domestic or international markets. In many areas, your decision will be limited to varying degrees by local content laws which designate that a certain percentage of goods and services must be bought locally. There is no question, however, that offshore procurement requires a complete investigation of global sourcing to be cost-effective. The same holds true for specialized products. You must remember, of course, that when you purchase from international sources that the price alone is not reflective of your total cost. Keep in mind that there will be numerous other costs such as transportation, duty, customs and freight added to the purchase price. This may increase the total cost of the procured MRO supplies to a level higher than you would pay domestically.

There are also a number of logistic strategies available to you in which your supplier is given the capability of distributing or setting up a service facility right in your plant. Various agreements can be worked out. Another strategy goes under the name of stocking programs in which the supplier is responsible for maintaining control over inventory or the level of provided services in your plant according to some agreed-upon schedule. This strategy relieves your procurement function from overseeing large areas of your company's purchasing activities.

Paying Attention to the Pennies

The most effective way to focus on reducing costs is to get the support of your suppliers and the people in your own company. One

difficult area, for example, is the procurement of maintenance components. In many companies, employees order directly from the supplier
and not through Purchasing, where more control can be exerted for
lower prices, 100% quality and high service. We strongly suggest that
all of our clients let both groups participate in the development of
MRO procurement strategies. Early supplier involvement in the process is critical to your success as is internal support from all the areas
affected in your company. In Wayne Douchkoff's book, *People Empowerment: Achieving Success from Involvement* (PT Publications), he ad-
dresses a complete program for gaining the support of the entire
company in any team effort at continuous improvement.

Another tool is the total cost approach which is not dependent
upon price analysis as the only criterion for determining the costs of
MRO goods and services. Cost analysis, on the other hand, examines
all the costs involved in their procurement. In order to achieve success
with this approach, it may be necessary for you to reengineer your cost
accounting system to incorporate life cycle accounting. The key ingre-
dient in long-term cost improvement is the analysis of all costs associ-
ated with MRO products and services.

Cost improvement cannot be restricted to any one area or commodity that you purchase. You need to look for other areas of opportunity. Nothing should be exempt from the cost improvement effort.
Driving cost improvement throughout the organization will require
an improved cost reporting system. You will need to add elements of
cost to financial reporting in order to expand your visibility. We
recommend the following categories of cost for MRO procurement:

MRO WORLD CLASS COST CATEGORIES (COST DRIVERS)

> **Quality — Preventive, Appraisal, Failure**
> **Inventory Transaction**
> **Processing — Cycle Time**
> **Maintenance — Cycle Time**
> **Support — Customer Service**

Included in these categories would be the actual cost elements which need to be collected and reported in order to reflect improvements. Product cost elements have traditionally supported material, labor and overhead measurements. Although material and labor are readily identifiable components of product cost, overhead represents a "catch-all" category for other costs. To be truly successful, cost systems must break down the components of overhead into elements of product cost that are meaningful at the operational level. Meaningful is the key word here. By "meaningful," we mean that the elements of cost must represent activities which are actually being performed and which therefore represent opportunities for improvement.

Awareness of these elements helps employees seek methods to eliminate or reduce cost elements. Workers who are tracking these costs can actually watch them add up and see which activities are contributing the most costs. The more team members in your company who understand this process of identifying the elements of cost, the better able they will be to assist in reducing activities.

We have found the following steps to be very effective in targeting and reducing costs in the procurement of MRO goods and services:

9-STEP COST IMPROVEMENT METHOD

1.   **Identify Targets and Opportunities**
2.   **Describe Them in Detail**
3.   **Identify and Define Possible Problems**
4.   **Set Objectives and Goals**
5.   **Gather Facts and other Related Information and Analyze the Data**
6.   **Determine Solutions**
7.   **Evaluate Solutions and Alternatives**
8.   **Implement Techniques to Solve Problems**
9.   **Evaluate and Measure Results**

The supplier's Cost of Quality (COQ) is a subject of wide interest as evidenced by the large amount of material which has been written for internal use on the topic and by the large number of companies becoming involved in Total Quality Management (TQM) programs. There are also a number of well-publicized quality prizes, such as the Deming and Baldrige awards, which keep interest in quality high. However, the awards are only in the categories of service, small business and manufacturing. There are no categories for MRO, distribution or freight suppliers. And lastly, there is the ISO 9000 which has established quality systems criteria which companies must meet in order to trade. All of this activity forms a good foundation upon which companies can initiate efforts to address total cost issues in MRO procurement.

Unfortunately, many companies do not understand COQ internally and how important it is to organizational results. COQ is not just the capturing of nonconformance data such as scrap, unfavorable yields and rework. Each buyer must also use COQ to measure the relationship between dollars spent due to the lack of quality and dollars spent on prevention or corrective cost in solving quality issues.

Inventory

Organizations measure inventory in a number of ways—inventory dollars, inventory turns, obsolescence dollars, slow moving dollars, and days, weeks or months of inventory. Although these measurements arrive at figures, they are not accurate or thorough enough for a total cost management system because none of them capture the cost of carrying inventory. For instance, some accounting systems use a 2% a month or 24% a year figure as a default to the Cost of Inventory (COI). It has been our experience, however, that most of our clients's COI is higher and that the drivers of inventory costs need to be identified. In fact, we have consistently noticed that the COI at our clients ranges between 25% and 45%. The numbers tell the story. A measurement for the carrying cost of inventory must be calculated and analyzed.

The categories of COI should include:

- **Storage Space.**
- **Handling and Equipment.**
- **Inventory Risk.**
- **Taxes and Service.**
- **Capital Cost.**

Tools for the Bottom Line

Lastly, we leave you with some tools for the MRO procurement bottom line. In today's highly competitive marketplace, companies must explore every opportunity to improve their competitive advantage. Continuous improvement is the key to success in this environment. In order to make substantial progress on the road to improvement, you must first measure and take stock of where you are. Purchasing performance measurements provide you with this information by establishing a benchmark, a baseline, a current status, and a starting point.

You can then identify both the strong and weak points of MRO procurement and develop action plans for improvement. With clearly defined goals/objectives in mind, you can use purchasing performance measurements to track improvement and to identify areas requiring corrective action.

You can keep on track with your initiative by keeping the following performance questions in mind:

What is performance?
What is performing? What is not performing?
What is the action required?
What is the follow-up action?
What is the benchmark?
When will it be done?
Who is responsible?

Another tool in your MRO initiative is benchmarking which can be used to identify and emulate those companies who already excel at

MRO procurement. Be aware, however, that this may not be cost-effective for you. It depends on your volume. In essence, the use of benchmarking allows you to form or improve upon your own company's methods of operation by taking certain practices from Company X and another set of practices from Company Y and applying them. Benchmarking is intended to provide opportunities to make breakthrough improvements in addition to incremental improvements through the continuous improvement process as shown in *Re-Engineering through Cycle Time Management* (PT Publications).

The rationale behind benchmarking is that the competition in today's marketplace is evolving at an ever increasing rate. The static targets that you may have once used are no longer effective. New markets are opening and closing faster than many companies can follow. The only way to keep ahead is to leapfrog over the competition by identifying and emulating the leading-edge practices of companies who are best-in-class. This *rarely* means emulating the practices of an entire company. What you will be doing is studying the practices of one department or function of the benchmarked company and an entirely different department or function in another company. Look beyond you own industry for companies to benchmark. The idea is to use the best of the best in designing your own organization. We mention this so that each buyer at every level can learn how to take responsibility for applying this tool.

Like the Continuous Improvement Process, benchmarking is also a continuous process. You should always be searching for companies which are performing better than your company and conducting a comparison to see what can be learned. There is always some organization you can learn from and that company may be in an industry totally unrelated to your own.

Process mapping, as discussed in *Power Purchasing: Supply Management in the 21st Century* (PT Publications), is another tool that companies can use to focus on managing and reducing the time it takes to complete a process or set of activities. Motorola has used process mapping since the early 1980s and its results have been remarkable. The company has witnessed a reduction of lead time for delivery of some products that went from eight weeks to four days. It is a good idea to deploy this technique to enhance a new buyer's learning process.

All of the strategies in this chapter can be prioritized based on return on investment, impact on customers, competitive advantage, lower cost through higher quality, ease of implementation, increased speed and flexibility, and so on. However they are drawn up, action plans are implemented by the teams that created the maps.

IDENTIFICATION

CHAPTER TWO

The point of developing an MRO procurement process is to increase your company's profitability. Companies placing a great deal of emphasis on supply management within their organization can expect significant improvement. One of our clients, ABB (Asea Brown Boveri), reports that saving 5% from reducing purchasing costs can have up to a 50% effect on profits. At another client, Motorola, they have evolved a purchasing organization characterized by commodity management teams and commodity specialists. They form the backbone of Motorola's logistic reorganization and a key part of its supply management strategy.

MRO procurement begins with the identification of MRO commodities — maintenance, repair and operating supplies — within your company. Further commodity separation is accomplished by using the following categories: Class, risk, bulk, type and critical success factors. Figure 2-1 shows how commodities can be identified and separated using this scheme.

Commodity	M	R	O	Class	Risk	Bulk	Type	Critical Success Factors

Figure 2-1.

Commodity Management Teams

It is the responsibility of commodity management teams to over-see the selection, qualification and certification of MRO suppliers. The commodity management team takes the approach of determining, by commodity codes and product types, how many suppliers are required by category and in aggregate as shown in Figure 2-2. Using this approach, the team can determine how much of the existing supply base should be retained and how many new suppliers are needed.

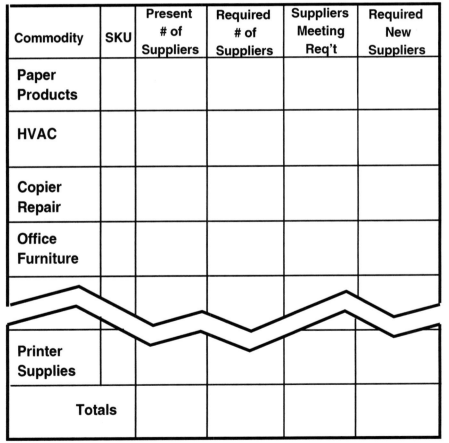

Commodity	SKU	Present # of Suppliers	Required # of Suppliers	Suppliers Meeting Req't	Required New Suppliers
Paper Products					
HVAC					
Copier Repair					
Office Furniture					
Printer Supplies					
Totals					

Figure 2-2.

One of our clients, Hydro Agri Europe (HAE), recently went about breaking down its suppliers by commodity and product type. When HAE began its commodity management process, there were thousands of suppliers. They are presently working to cut suppliers significantly by applying the supplier selection criteria they had previously developed to their current supply base. You should be undertaking a similar process for your MRO purchases.

Sector Sourcing Organization

In addition to forming commodity management teams, Motorola has organized its business sectors so that they are better able to meet the regional and divisional demands of supply management. Their mission reads as follows:

SECTOR SOURCING MISSION

Provide and execute strategic sourcing plans that enhance the sector's total customer satisfaction efforts through commodity expertise in technology, quality and responsiveness.

All the sectors also had similar strategic thrusts which are outlined below and adapted for use by all types of companies:

STRATEGIC THRUSTS

1) **To seek out, develop and utilize global "Best-In-Class" suppliers for all commodities.**

2) **To develop with our suppliers a total quality culture that institutionalizes the process of Six Sigma in all our commodity processes and procedures.**

3) **To improve our responsiveness to customers through the continuous reduction of our procurement cycle time, resulting in 100% on-time supplier performance.**

---

4) **To leverage commodity procurement and develop proactive, cooperative relationships, resulting in improved financial results in our profit margins.**

5) **To develop and implement sourcing plans that insure long-term partnerships between the company and its MRO suppliers and optimal performance.**

As you can see, the goals of Motorola were ambitious and the company needed the strategy above to bring them to fruition. The overall objectives of this strategy are to improve communications between your company and its MRO suppliers, to improve the performance of your business and to share mutual growth opportunities with your MRO suppliers.

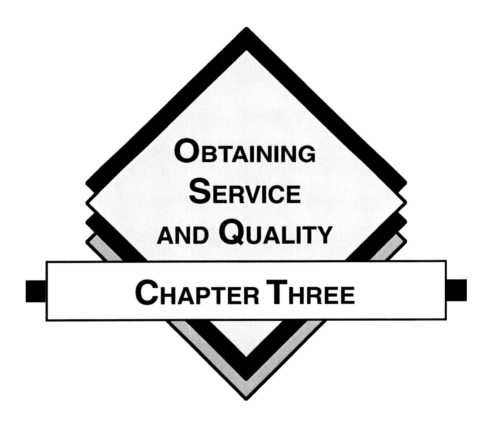

OBTAINING

SERVICE

AND QUALITY

CHAPTER THREE

The level of customer service you should expect from an MRO supplier is the same as the level from all suppliers—100% satisfaction. At the minimum, this means on-time delivery, quality service and material, and guaranteed equipment up-time. Supplier requirements should consistently be expanded to include condition-based monitoring so that the partner can meet its uptime objectives. It should also include the presence of emergency service lines to the supplier and sufficient inventory levels for spares. Furthermore, the supplier should be utilizing SPC (Statistical Process Control) in their administrative and logistical areas to ensure the levels of 100% quality. Quality of service and cost will be the principal factors used in differentiating suppliers in the future.

Customer Satisfaction

All too often, companies accept that customer satisfaction cannot be measured quantitatively. Instead, they rely on their perceptions and "feel-good" guesses, rather than facts. We believe that your customer satisfaction with suppliers can be made into a comparative measure which identifies what you are spending to achieve satisfaction versus the identifiable costs of not being satisfied. Let's look at customer delivery cycle time performance as an example of how you can improve your customer satisfaction. First, here are the measurements you need to take:

- **What percentage of your MRO supplier's deliveries are on-time? ___%**

- **How many past due orders are there in terms of dollars ___ and line items ___?**

- **How long does it take to complete a request for receipt? ___**

- **How much have cycle times been reduced? ___**

Then map and measure their actual shipping time and the order cycle time against the date required by your company. This measurement should be broken down by supplier, service and product in order to detect where problems are occurring. We advocate that you establish a goal of a 100% service level to your request date. Once established, you measure actual shipping versus the shipping plan on a monthly, quarterly and year-to-date schedule. Remember to include past due orders which should be rolled forward into the current month. Your MRO supplier's performance should be measured on the sum of past due orders and the current month which will require them to make up the backlog as well as the current month's orders.

It is also vital for your company to measure the total scope of customer satisfaction. While measurements in this area are sometimes imprecise, they are essential in providing a litmus test of performance in the marketplace. Measurements should include:

1. **Number of complaints against orders shipped** _____

2. **Warranty claims**

   Number of occurrences by type/by MRO supplier _____

   Number of reoccurrences by type/by MRO supplier _____

   Warranty dollars $_____

   Number of repairs by age category of the product _____

3. **Unquantified measurements**

   Market surveys on performance (quality, delivery, function, etc.)

4. **Are other functional areas, besides customer service, used to survey/contact MRO suppliers?**   ____Yes ____No

5. **How would you describe your reputation with the majority of your MRO suppliers?**

   _____
   _____
   _____
   _____
   _____

The preceding questions will provide you with suggestions as to where you can start to improve customer satisfaction. Companies often assume that nothing can be done to improve customer service and satisfaction in these areas, but they are very wrong if they accept that assumption as true. Here is another survey you can use to evaluate the strength of your partnerships with suppliers (a score of 1 indicates poor performance; a score of 6 indicates superior performance):

A.	Supplier Involvement in Planning	1 2 3 4 5 6
B.	Negotiation and Award Process	1 2 3 4 5 6
C.	Schedule Sharing with EDI Release	1 2 3 4 5 6
D.	Schedule Stability — Window of Opportunity	1 2 3 4 5 6
E.	Technical Support — Sales and Engineering	1 2 3 4 5 6
F.	Technology Sharing	1 2 3 4 5 6
G.	Quality Initiatives	1 2 3 4 5 6
H.	Cycle Time Reduction Initiatives	1 2 3 4 5 6
I.	Response to Cost Reduction Ideas	1 2 3 4 5 6
J.	Identification of Cost Drivers	1 2 3 4 5 6
K.	Business Growth Potential	1 2 3 4 5 6
L.	Profitability	1 2 3 4 5 6
M.	Professionalism in Conducting Supplier Surveys	1 2 3 4 5 6
N.	Purchasing Professionalism	1 2 3 4 5 6
O.	Communications and Feedback	1 2 3 4 5 6
P.	Training and Education Effectiveness	1 2 3 4 5 6
Q.	Preferred Status	1 2 3 4 5 6
R.	Partnership for Growth Program	1 2 3 4 5 6
S.	Management Commitment to Partnership	1 2 3 4 5 6

Ratings of this type will give you a good idea of how well you are managing your supply base.

Selecting Distributors and OEMs

In Chapter One, we provided several major areas of criteria which you can use when surveying MRO distributors and OEMs (Original Equipment Manufacturers). These criteria need to be put into a survey format which will allow you to collect information critical to supply management. On the following pages, we have provided you with two examples — an MRO supplier survey and a distributor survey.

Each survey consists of a Survey Scoring Summary and several sections covering an individual area such as Total Quality Management, Housekeeping or Process Management.

Both of the surveys are preceded by a tool called an Evaluation Criteria Point Value. We evaluate suppliers by assigning a point value to each of the criterion in our supplier survey and audit form. The purpose of this procedure is to objectively quantify a supplier's capabilities in order to fairly and accurately document the current level of operations. We feel that the use of the point values listed in our tool assures suppliers of consistent, unbiased evaluations.

The buyer or team would conduct the survey in this chapter by visiting the distributor or MRO supplier and interviewing appropriate people. The questions in each section would be asked and the responses noted. Any additional comments can be added at the end of each section. Scores can be added at the time of the survey or later when the team has time to sit down and evaluate the information they have gathered. Scores are then added up and placed in the summaries.

Evaluation Criteria Point Value			
Question Score	Approach	Deployment	Results
0 Poor	• No system evident • No management recognition evident	• None	• Anecdotal
2 Weak	• Beginnings of system/process • Limited resource commitment	• Some activities started • Deployment in some areas	• Some evidence of output • Limited results
4 Fair	• Prevention-based system defined • Less than total mgmt. support	• Deployed in some major areas and some support areas	• Inconsistent, but positive results
6 Approved	• Sound system in place with evidence of evaluation/ improvement cycles • Some evidence of business integration • Proactive leadership emerging	• Deployed in most major areas and some support areas • Mostly consistent and accepted	• Positive trends in most areas • Evidence that results caused by approach
8 Qualified	• Well-designed system/ process with evidence of Continuous Improvement Program • Good to excellent integration • Total mgmt. support	• Consistent across all major areas and most support areas • Consistent and pervasive acceptance	• Positive trends and known results • All requirements met
10 Excellent	• Systematic prevention that anticipates customer needs • Total management leadership and commitment • Publicly acknowledged and industry recognized	• Consistent across all major areas and support areas • All operations	• Excellent, sustained results • Exceeds requirements • World Class

MRO SUPPLIER
SURVEY AND AUDIT FORM

Date _____

Supplier Company

Address

Survey Contact Person   Name
                            Phone
                            Fax

Survey/Audit Team   Supply Leader

Survey Scoring Summary

	Selection Category	Total Points Avail.	Points Awarded	Weight Factor	Score
1	Organization	100	_____	.10	_____
2	Product/Service	100	_____	.25	_____
3	Quality Management	100	_____	.25	_____
4	Service Management	100	_____	.20	_____
5	Customer Satisfaction	100	_____	.20	_____
		500		1.00	

TOTAL SCORE   _____

CATEGORY 1: Organization

		Yes	No	PTS

1. Does the supplier have a well defined and documented organizational structure? ___ ___ ___
2. Does management support a partnership relationship with customers and suppliers? ___ ___ ___
3. Is there an ongoing commitment to reducing cycle time in areas such as order handling, administration and handling of complaints? ___ ___ ___
4. Is there a policy for hiring people with adequate education and skills? ___ ___ ___
5. Has the supplier implemented employee education and training programs to meet customer requirements and quality targets? ___ ___ ___
6. Does the supplier have a follow-up procedure for updating changes in governmental regulations? ___ ___ ___
7. Has the supplier begun implementation of Electronic Data Interchange (EDI)? ___ ___ ___

TOTAL POINTS:

POINTS AWARDED (Total Points X 1.43):
(Record in "Points Awarded" column of Survey Scoring Summary)

Comments:

CATEGORY 2: Product/Service

		Yes	No	PTS

1. Does the supplier have a policy for the development of new products/services? ___ ___ ___
2. Has the supplier properly documented the development process to ensure consistent reproducibility? ___ ___ ___
3. Does the supplier include customer requirements in the development of new products/services? ___ ___ ___
4. Are there specific quality objectives in place for the development of new products/services? ___ ___ ___
5. Does the supplier maintain adequate records about approved materials sources? ___ ___ ___

6. Is there a procedure for recording quality and dates of incoming material? ___ ___ ___
7. Do packing materials conform to environmental requirements? ___ ___ ___
8. Will the supplier accept the return of material, including packaging? ___ ___ ___
9. Does the supplier use the proper identification labels on each parcel of the shipment? ___ ___ ___
10. Do the markings include reference codes and other data that the customer requires? ___ ___ ___
11. Is there a detailed written procedure outlining the shipment of products? ___ ___ ___
12. Has the supplier documented the methods for shipping hazardous material and made them well understood? ___ ___ ___
13. Does the supplier have bar coding capability? ___ ___ ___

TOTAL POINTS:

POINTS AWARDED (Total Points X .769):
(Record in "Points Awarded" column of Survey Scoring Summary)

Comments:

CATEGORY 3: Quality Management

		Yes	No	PTS

1. Does the supplier hold regular management reviews? ___ ___ ___
2. Are quality issues such as customer satisfaction, quality cost, and audit reviews handled at reviews? ___ ___ ___
3. Does the supplier follow up on corrective actions during the review meetings? ___ ___ ___
4. Is there a long-term quality improvement plan? ___ ___ ___
5. Does the supplier follow the implementation of this plan during review meetings? ___ ___ ___
6. Has management released a written quality policy/commitment? ___ ___ ___
7. Is this quality policy/commitment communicated to the whole organization? ___ ___ ___
8. Has management explained what the policy means to the work of each employee? ___ ___ ___
9. Does the supplier regularly update the quality policy? ___ ___ ___

10. Does the supplier have a clearly defined quality function for supporting quality directives? ___ ___ ___
11. Does the supplier have a system of measuring quality performance? ___ ___ ___
12. Does the supplier base its corrective actions on these quality metrics? ___ ___ ___

TOTAL POINTS:

POINTS AWARDED (Total Points X .833):
(Record in "Points Awarded" column of Survey Scoring Summary)

Comments:

CATEGORY 4: Service Management

Yes No PTS

1. Does the supplier maintain written safety instruction for its products and services? ___ ___ ___
2. Do the written instructions take into account occupational health and safety regulations? ___ ___ ___
3. Are the handling instructions and controls for hazardous materials correct and up to date? ___ ___ ___
4. Is the corrective action system based on safety records? ___ ___ ___
5. Does the supplier advocate a policy of cross-training and personnel rotation? ___ ___ ___
6. Does the supplier have a system for immediate responses to urgent needs for repairs/services/products? ___ ___ ___
7. Has the supplier named a contact person for each of its customers? ___ ___ ___

TOTAL POINTS:

POINTS AWARDED (Total Points X 1.43):
(Record in "Points Awarded" column of Survey Scoring Summary)

Comments:

CATEGORY 5: Customer Satisfaction

Yes No PTS

1. Does the supplier have a system for effectively measuring
    customer satisfaction levels with the company's total
    performance?   ___ ___ ___
2. Are independent surveys of competitors used to
    benchmark customer satisfaction results?   ___ ___ ___
3. Does the supplier have both internal and external goals
    forachieving Total Customer Satisfaction?   ___ ___ ___
4. Is the goal of 100% customer satisfaction understood
    by all levels of the organization?   ___ ___ ___
5. Does the supplier make sure that plans for customer
    satisfaction are implemented?   ___ ___ ___
6. Does the supplier have a system for handling customer
    relationships and complaints?   ___ ___ ___
7. Does the supplier have a system for determining future
    requirements and expectations of customers?   ___ ___ ___

TOTAL POINTS:

POINTS AWARDED (Total Points X 1.43):
(Record in "Points Awarded" column of Survey Scoring Summary)

Comments:

MRO DISTRIBUTOR
SURVEY AND AUDIT FORM

Date _____

Supplier Company

Address

Survey Contact Person   Name
                               Phone
                               Fax

Survey / Audit Team   Supply Leader

Survey Scoring Summary

	Selection Category	Total Points Avail.	Points Awarded	Weight Factor	Score
1	Quality Management	100	_____	.15	_____
2	Administration	100	_____	.10	_____
3	Supply Management	100	_____	.25	_____
4	Storage Management	100	_____	.10	_____
5	Logistics	100	_____	.20	_____
6	Customer Satisfaction	100	_____	.20	_____
		600		1.00	

TOTAL SCORE_____

CATEGORY 1: Quality Management

	Yes	No	PTS
1. Does the distributor hold regular management reviews?	___	___	___
2. Are quality issues such as customer satisfaction, on-time delivery, delivery quality and audit reports handled at reviews?	___	___	___
3. Does the distributor follow up on corrective actions during the review meetings?	___	___	___
4. Has management released a written quality policy/ commitment?	___	___	___
5. Is this quality policy/commitment communicated to the whole organization?	___	___	___
6. Has management explained what the policy means to the work of each employee?	___	___	___
7. Does the distributor regularly update the quality policy?	___	___	___
8. Does the distributor have a documented quality assurance system?	___	___	___
9. Does the distributor have a clearly defined quality function for supporting quality directives?	___	___	___
10. Are responsibilities clear, known and documented?	___	___	___
11. Does the distributor have an ongoing quality training program for all personnel?	___	___	___
12. Is the QA system certified by a third party?	___	___	___
13. Does the distributor have a system for basing corrective actions on customer feedback?	___	___	___
14. Does the distributor have a system of measuring on-time performance, delivery quality, etc.?	___	___	___
15. Does the distributor base its corrective actions on these quality metrics?	___	___	___

TOTAL POINTS:

POINTS AWARDED (Total Points X .667):
(Record in "Points Awarded" column of Survey Scoring Summary)

Comments:

CATEGORY 2: Administration

	Yes	No	PTS
1. Does the distributor have a well defined and documented organizational structure?	___	___	___
2. Does management support a partnership relationship with customers and suppliers?	___	___	___
3. Is the distributor receptive to new ideas and changes for continuous quality improvement?	___	___	___
4. Is there an ongoing commitment to reducing cycle time in areas such as order handling, administration and handling of complaints?	___	___	___
5. Does the distributor use an internal interest rate in its cost accounting?	___	___	___
6. Does the distributor split total cost into different categories and is it willing to share this information with customers?	___	___	___
7. Has the distributor communicated its goals on quality, costs, and customer satisfaction to all employees?	___	___	___
8. Is area performance reported to both management and employees on a regular basis?	___	___	___
9. Does the distributor's management sufficiently support ongoing training and is it documented by an organizational training plan?	___	___	___
10. Does the distributor provide a quality education training program for all employees?	___	___	___
11. Does the distributor provide training in the principles of Time-Based Management?	___	___	___
12. Are administrative quality systems given equal importance as product/service quality systems?	___	___	___
13. Does the distributor's cost accounting system split cost data into different cost categories for preliminary calculations and actual data?	___	___	___
14. Is the cost of quality system effective and does it lead to corrective actions?	___	___	___
15. Does the distributor have a back-up system for computer systems, files and documents?	___	___	___

TOTAL POINTS:

POINTS AWARDED (Total Points X .667):
(Record in "Points Awarded" column of Survey Scoring Summary)

Comments:

CATEGORY 3: Supply Management

Yes No PTS

1. Is a Supplier Selection and Certification program in place? ___ ___ ___
2. Has the distributor established partnership agreements? ___ ___ ___
3. Does the distributor keep adequate records of approved
    sources? ___ ___ ___
4. Has the distributor established quality metrics and
    improvement goals in conjunction with its suppliers? ___ ___ ___
5. Are suppliers rated and informed about their
    performance? ___ ___ ___
6. Does the distributor use qualified people to
    audit suppliers? ___ ___ ___
7. Is data available about the supplier's process
    capabilities? ___ ___ ___
8. Are supplier's materials clearly specified and
    documented? ___ ___ ___
9. Does the distributor have a system for informing
    customers about supplier specification changes? ___ ___ ___
10. Is there a written procedure for receiving materials? ___ ___ ___
11. Does the distributor have a procedure for recording
    incoming quantities and dates? ___ ___ ___
12. Does the distributor adequately protect incoming
    material from the environment? ___ ___ ___
13. Is there a procedure which is followed that fully
    confirms the purchase order and specifications
    of incoming material? ___ ___ ___
14. Are the procedures for identifying and tracing distributed
    materials adequate? ___ ___ ___
15. Is information about supplier testing procedures
    available? ___ ___ ___
16. Does the distributor monitor test results from
    the suppliers? ___ ___ ___
17. Is there a corrective action system for nonconforming
    material? ___ ___ ___
18. Is nonconforming material properly segregated from
    approved material? ___ ___ ___

TOTAL POINTS:

POINTS AWARDED (Total Points X .556):
(Record in "Points Awarded" column of Survey Scoring Summary)

Comments:

CATEGORY 4: Storage Management

                                                            Yes No PTS

1. Does the distributor keep lots intact and traceable through
    the entire material chain?   ___ ___ ___
2. Is there a system for identifying which materials are
    approved or rejected?   ___ ___ ___
3. Does the distributor properly identify and segregate
    nonconforming material from qualified material?   ___ ___ ___
4. Is the receipt, handling, storage, packaging and release of
    all material specified and controlled to prevent damage,
    deterioration and obsolescence?   ___ ___ ___
5. Are only authorized personnel able to store and retrieve
    material?   ___ ___ ___
6. Does the distributor handle important documents properly
    and protect them adequately?   ___ ___ ___
7. Is there a written procedure and distribution list for
    communicating changes to documents?   ___ ___ ___
8. Does the distributor remove obsolete drawings and
    specifications from use?   ___ ___ ___
9. Are current documents free of handwritten and unofficial
    changes?   ___ ___ ___
10. Does the distributor have procedures and documents for
    proper storage and inventory control of hazardous
    materials?   ___ ___ ___
11. Are timely and effective corrective actions taken that are
    based on records of work injuries and absences?   ___ ___ ___
12. Is there a shelf-life program for distributed products? ___ ___ ___
13. Is there a written safety manual?   ___ ___ ___
14. Is the facility kept clean and free of all non-essential items?___ ___
15. Does the distributor have a written procedure for electrostatic
    discharge protection when electrical components are used?___ ___
16. Does the distributor have a procedure for informing
    customers of out-of-stock or discontinued products?   ___ ___ ___

TOTAL POINTS:

POINTS AWARDED (Total Points X .625):
(Record in "Points Awarded" column of Survey Scoring Summary)

Comments:

CATEGORY 5: Logistics

	Yes	No	PTS
1. Does the distributor maintain packaging specifications?	___	___	___
2. Are there written procedures for packaging the product?	___	___	___
3. Do the procedures permit the definition of packaging by customers?	___	___	___
4. Do the packaging materials conform to environmental regulations?	___	___	___
5. Does the distributor accept the return of material, including packaging material?	___	___	___
6. Does a written procedure exist for marking containers for shipping?	___	___	___
7. Does the distributor use the proper identification labels for each container that is shipped?	___	___	___
8. Do these markings include reference codes and other data supplied by the customer?	___	___	___
9. Does the distributor have written procedures outlining the details of shipping a product?	___	___	___
10. Does the distributor have bar coding capability?	___	___	___
11. Are customer routing instructions visible on packages? Are traffic and routing guides maintained in the shipping department?	___	___	___
12. Has the distributor ensured that the methods for shippinghazardous material are fully documented and understood?	___	___	___
13. Is the responsibility for company logistics clearly defined?	___	___	___
14. Does the distributor have procedures for handling non-received material?	___	___	___
15. Will the distributor deliver directly to the customer's production line?	___	___	___
16. Is the distributor capable of EDI (Electronic Data Interchange)?	___	___	___
17. If the distributor is not using EDI, do they have definite plans for its introduction?	___	___	___

TOTAL POINTS:

POINTS AWARDED (Total Points X .588):
(Record in "Points Awarded" column of Survey Scoring Summary)

Comments:

	Yes	No	PTS
1. Does the distributor have a system for effectively measuringcustomer satisfaction levels with the company's total performance?	___	___	___
2. Are independent surveys of competitors used to benchmark `customer satisfaction results?	___	___	___
3. Does the distributor have both internal and external goals for achieving Total Customer Satisfaction?	___	___	___
4. Is the goal of 100% customer satisfaction understood by all levels of the organization?	___	___	___
5. Does the distributor make sure that plans for customer satisfaction are implemented?	___	___	___
6. Does the distributor have a system for handling customer relationships and complaints?	___	___	___
7. Does the distributor have a system for determining future requirements and expectations of customers?	___	___	___

TOTAL POINTS:

POINTS AWARDED (Total Points X 1.43):
(Record in "Points Awarded" column of Survey Scoring Summary)

Comments:

Internal vs. External Sources

In the MRO area, we frequently find a situation where a company must decide whether to make or buy an item. To decide which course to take, you should investigate the market rate for the the purchase and delivery of that item from external sources. Don't forget to consider the prices and costs from suppliers with whom you have an extended program. Their costs can be significantly lower. Then, you should calculate the cost to service the product or perform the service in-house. Internal costs should include the following:

- **Labor rate.**
- **Skill level required.**
- **Cost of workforce.**
- **Facility cost.**
- **Facility capacity to deliver the item.**
- **Customer service.**
- **Overhead structure. (Compared to supply base structure.)**
- **Cost of quality.**
- **Cost of inventory.**
- **Freight/transportation.**

Calculating internal costs can be complicated and difficult to compare with outside suppliers. When performing a "make or buy" analysis, the MRO buyer should fully examine why the supplier is quoting that particular price. A higher price might be acceptable if it meets all your requirements. The objective is to find out which course of action will cost less, why it will cost less, and for how long will it cost less.

Most important of all, determine who is the highest quality producer today and who is most likely to continue to be the highest quality producer in the future. Cost reduction begins with a plan of what your maximum and minimum levels will be. Set these levels and go into negotiation with a clear idea of what you are willing to pay.

Power, Information and Time

When purchasing MRO supplies, maintenance and repairs, negotiation over OEM vs. non-OEM product is of paramount importance. Other important negotiation issues are stock levels, inventory reduction and planned vs. unplanned orders. Whatever you are negotiating for with a supplier, the three major elements of the negotiation process are power, time and information. Without these three items working side by side, real negotiation will not happen.

There are several ways to make power work for you. First, you should recognize and evaluate your opponent, the person with whom you are negotiating in the context of the competition. If there is a lot of competition in the arena, then you immediately have more power. If there is less competition, then your perceived power may be diminished. But there are ways to preserve power even in a sole source situation. We refer you to the audiotape, *The World of Negotiations: How to Win Every Time* (PT Publications) for a practical guide to negotiation in business.

Learn as much as possible about the products you want to buy. Include gathering information about the product in your negotiation strategy. Many salespeople know little about the product they are selling. They don't know how it is made or how it works. All they know is that it costs $1.00 and comes in red or blue. If you find out that this

MIL

- **MUST achieve.**

- **INTEND to achieve.**

- **Would LIKE to achieve.**

is the extent of their knowledge, you might be at a distinct advantage if you have completed your homework in preparing for the negotiations. Knowledge will keep power on your side.

Before you begin negotiations, we suggest that you write out clear objectives. One way to make certain they are clearly defined is to use the MIL approach. The initials stand for objectives you:

Before entering into any negotiation, we strongly suggest that you write down realistic objectives. Complete Figure 3-1 for a specific product or commodity you currently purchase. Use the MIL column to make reasonable guesses about what your supplier is looking for. Again, we want to emphasize that a plan must be prepared with a strategy that includes the MIL objectives. Each plan should include what you are willing to give, your fallback positions and your order of counter-offers.

	Date _____						
Product Purchased: _____							
Supplier: _____							
By: _____ **Date:** _____							

Goals	**My MIL**			**Supplier MIL**			**What I'm Willing to Give**
	M	**I**	**L**	**M**	**I**	**L**	
Quantity							
Quality							
Price							
Delivery							
Terms/Conditions							
Life of Contract							
Payment Terms							
Alternate/Substitute							
Cost Reduction Efforts							
Inventory							
Cost							

Figure 3-1.

Phone Negotiations

Special attention must be paid to phone negotiations in MRO purchasing since it is the most frequently used method of conducting business. Although phone negotiations are generally shorter in duration and involve smaller sums of money, they do alter bargaining. You should be aware that the phone offers opportunities as well as disadvantages. You can use the phone, for example, to control timing in negotiations. If you don't want to talk at any particular time, you don't need to take the call. Or, if the negotiations aren't going well, you can claim a bad connection or cut things short due to some other interruption in your office. They even have a gadget on the market now which creates the sounds of static, phone ringing or paging. In phone negotiations, you have a built-in buffer which can give you the edge.

On the other hand, because there is no visual contact whereby you can read facial expressions and body language, using the phone can lead to misunderstandings such as making unwarranted assumptions or failing to address the other person's needs. These errors often occur because negotiators usually fail to prepare as thoroughly as they would for face to face negotiations. They also occur because it is easy to assume something is understood. This assumption could be fatal. Never assume that anything is understood. A good way to avoid this situation is to ask the other person to explain himself, to repeat what he means or what he thinks you have told him. Try to be more precise yourself in the words you choose and, above all, listen much more carefully. You should follow up a phone call with a letter of confirmation.

Another way to lessen the chances of confusion is to approach phone negotiations with careful preparation. Make a list of specific issue in advance and know what you will and won't accept. Make sure you don't leave anything out by trying a dry run. Go through the upcoming phone conversation in your mind and try to anticipate all the contingencies. Adopt the motto of the Boy Scouts and "Be Prepared!" Misunderstandings are all to often at the root of badly negotiated deals, lawsuits and downed production lines.

MANAGING INVENTORIES

CHAPTER FOUR

Like other types of inventory, MRO supplies can tie up a company's assets. This is especially true in capital-intensive industries where MRO inventory may actually be larger than product inventory. One of our clients had $16 million in MRO purchases out of $31 million of total purchases. Much of the effort expended in managing this inventory can be viewed as nonvalue-added. It is thus imperative that MRO purchasing personnel begin exploring alternative methods of inventory management, such as those coming under the umbrella of Cycle

Time Management as shown in Figure 4-1. For more information, refer to Wayne Douchkoff and Tom Petroski's book, *Reengineering Through Cycle Time Management* (PT Publications). Such inventory management has the following advantages and benefits:

1. **Improves your competitive position both domestically and internationally.**

2. **Eliminates waste (Inventory, Carrying Costs, Physical Space, Material Handling, etc.).**

3. **Exposes unproductive processes.**

4. **Minimizes obsolescence.**

5. **Introduces flexibility.**

6. **Allows a company to respond more quickly to change.**

7. **Permits quick response to customer demands.**

The intent of cycle time reduction is to get the right material to the right place at the right time so that every procedure and operation adds value to your company's products and services. The goal of cycle time reduction is to produce or provide in one day all the products or services you need in order to fill customer orders. This will result in less material in the facility since inventory will not sit in storage or queues, adding carrying costs to your bottom line.

This method of MRO inventory management runs counter to the prevailing attitude that companies need safety stocks. Such inventory, however, only solves one problem at the expense of covering up far more serious problems. On the other hand, eliminating high levels of inventory has the important function of exposing hidden problems. Actually dealing with real problems and not hiding behind walls of inventory allows a company to be more flexible and productive.

As for MRO inventory accuracy, a cycle time reduction program not only allows you to locate inaccuracies, but to locate the sources of

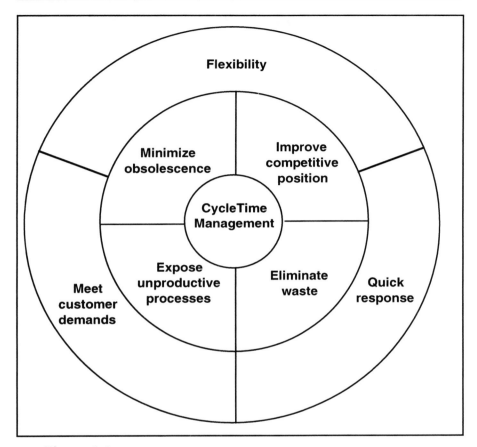

Figure 4-1.

inaccuracies. Then, you can eliminate the cause of the inaccuracy. You should examine whether this type of program can be applied to MRO inventories in your company. At one of our clients, a team using a similar program found that even though first shift maintenance personnel developed and maintained inventory controls, 75% of the parts were taken during the second and third shifts. Most maintenance people are not aware of what can be done in managing inventory levels and delivery. They want lots of material around, just-in-case. This same company had product in stores that was over 30 years old. This process of uncovering gaps in the flow of work in your company also affects inventory record accuracy. A good inventory management program makes the training and educating of employees in record accuracy a primary focus. Storeroom employees must know procedures which insure accuracy and require follow-up audits.

Getting MRO Supplies to the Point of Use

One of the objectives of MRO procurement is to get material directly to the point where it is needed, at just the moment it is needed, in the quantity it is needed. To reach this objective requires a supplier who is willing to work with you in the continuing battle against redundancy and waste. You can find such a supplier and establish a ship-to-WIP delivery objective by following these six steps:

1) **Select potential supplier — pay attention to its past quality control record and its complete quality control system.**

2) **Make an initial presentation to the supplier's management — begin convincing them of the merits of just-in-time delivery and 100% quality.**

3) **Initiate a complete and detailed supplier quality survey — you should be more concerned with the creation of long-range relationships with cooperative suppliers than with short-term relationships based on price.**

4) **Draft a basic, contractual agreement defining scope, purpose, implementation and responsibilities of customer and supplier.**

5) **Review and modify the plan — remember that the supplier is an expert in its field; seek their advice.**

6) **Establish an ongoing partnership.**

Point of Use Objectives

One of the methods by which you can get MRO supplies directly to the secretary or person making the requisition is use some variation of a Kanban system. This has the added benefit of greatly reducing paperwork. The purpose of a Kanban system is to signal a need. In fact, I address Kanban in *Made in America: The Total Business Concept* (PT

Publications), as a means to communicate. Kanban can communicate these signals throughout the different areas of an organization — administration, support, materials, manufacturing and service.

A Kanban card is used to signal a demand to trigger a pull internally through various operations and to signal a demand externally for replenishment. This combination of signal followed by replenishment continues throughout all of the operations and eventually to the company's suppliers who then replenish the consumed parts or services. Figure 4-2 shows an example of a typical Kanban pull system. This system can be made complete all the way to the supplier's site.

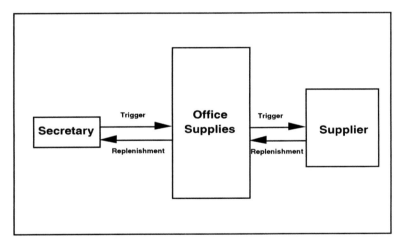

Figure 4-2.

MRO procurement should look upon Kanban systems as an excellent opportunity to cut administrative costs. If implemented and used properly, Kanban can eliminate most paper and manual transactions which add cost to the purchasing process. Kanban cards which make their way through operations eventually find their way to Purchasing to signal a reorder. All Purchasing needs to do with the card is to scan the bar code in order to create a release against a contract previously established with the supplier. The card is then put into an envelope and mailed to the supplier instead of a purchase order or, in the case of more sophisticated systems, an electronic data interchange (EDI) is performed. Upon receipt of the card, the supplier responds by shipping the appropriate part in the standard quantity printed on the card. The card is returned with the shipment of parts. Some companies use purchasing bank cards in a similar manner.

Purchasing cards are a relatively new phenomenon. They differ from regular credit cards in one important way. Controls can be placed on them so that they can be used only in a manner that your company desires. In other words, you can limit their use to certain items, suppliers and price ceilings. They also allow for the direct entry of orders to suppliers and direct billing and payment. As a result, they significantly reduce paperwork and costs. In a recent issue of *NAPM InfoEdge* on purchasing cards, the authors noted that a typical purchase order cost breakout adds up to $152. Compare that with the cost breakout of a purchasing card which amounts to $2-5.

Whatever method you use, you can expect the following savings from a Kanban or similar system:

- **No requisitions**
- **No order entry**
- **No purchase order**
- **No packing slip**
- **No receiving ticket**
- **No receipt transaction**
- **No stocking ticket**
- **No inventory update**
- **No invoice**

This short list alone has eliminated six forms and three manual transactions. Scanning the bar code on Kanban cards sends automatic updates to purchasing, inventory and financial files. One of our clients, ITT Barton, implemented a Kanban system for 20 part numbers at only one location on their plant floor. Three months after the implementation, the savings were recorded as over $50,000! Management had no problem authorizing the continuation of the Kanban project into other locations.

The New MRO Warehouse

There are a number of other MRO inventory replenishment systems, including bin stocking, supplier stocking, outsourcing programs, internal distribution and kitting programs. Many companies, of course, don't buy directly from manufacturers, but from distributors. How can they control the selection of suppliers in this situation? If you are a high volume buyer, you can exert control over the distributor's requirements put on each of its suppliers. If you aren't a high volume buyer, then you should make every effort to find distributors who have a rigorous selection process in place and who maintain an excellent quality profile and reputation. Future Electronics, a Massachusetts firm, has started a World Class program for distribution in which their customers can do one-stop shopping. The company's objective is to negotiate a win/win arrangement whereby their customers can purchase 100 percent of their electronic components from Future. In exchange, Future will supply kits of material as required (Just-In-Time).

In a recent meeting with Roland Dewberry, Director—Material Services, of Avnet-EMG in Arizona, he showed us how he has helped to establish and position Avnet for the future. They kit electronics from numerous suppliers (such as Motorola) for their customer base. This can be done in a similar manner for MRO procurement of items in all areas. An excellent area to start in order to gain experience is in the purchase of office supplies.

Speaking of office supplies, there is a company called Corporate Express, headquartered in Colorado, which is an excellent example of the type of MRO supplier to cultivate. They have over 100 locations with 34 warehouses. Besides offering services on how to design and configure office space for maximum productivity, they also provide electronic means for customized ordering, invoicing, reporting and tracking. Their stated objective is "to lower your company's overall procurement costs while providing exceptional service and the highest quality product." These are the goals that you want to see from all of your MRO suppliers.

A company with multiple divisions in different states should take advantage of the buying power of all its divisions by negotiating a system contract or National Agreement in aggregate. This is called cross-commodity leverage. A single division buying the same material or service and negotiating a purchase on its own has only a portion of the volume that the whole company has. Together, the team can negotiate better prices and contract terms. In the case of a decentralized company where each division or plant works independently, the purchaser in the plant with the highest volume should provide a lead negotiator for that commodity and let others feed off that arrangement. Concentrate on payment terms, terms and conditions, separating cost elements, and establishment of stocking locations.

Bar Coding

Bar coding helps to reduce inventory by maintaining the accuracy and timeliness of transactions. It can help with reordering when using visual order point systems. One of our clients requested that its supplier maintain inventory at the client's facility. This required that the salesperson visually check on-hand balances. They then implemented bar coding which allowed the salesperson to scan the below-order-point items. This created an electronic order that could be downloaded daily directly into the supplier's order entry system.

Use of Rationalized Inventory Management Techniques

Stocking levels are typically determined using "rule of thumb" principles, such as maintaining one month's supply. These rules, however, actually inflate overall inventory and very often do not reduce stockouts. Order points contain several principles which, when understood, can lead to reduced inventory and increased service level. Here are some of these principles:

- Items display different lead times and usage. Therefore, order points should be time specific.

- Safety stock is used to cover the times when usage varies. Therefore, items which display little variability require less safety stock added to the order point. The opposite is true also. Items with greater variability require higher safety stock levels.

- Variability is not always random. For example, one of our clients investigated the causes of variability and discovered two common sources that allowed them to reduce inventory, level demand on suppliers, and increase service levels. They found that approximately 40% of usage was for regularly scheduled preventive maintenance and could therefore be scheduled, not stocked. The second leading cause was lumpy (variable) demand patterns that reflected replenishment from the main inventory to departmental inventories. In other words, not true demand. Not so surprisingly, the actual demand patterns did not display much variability.

The ideal situation when it comes to managing MRO purchasing activities and contracts is to eliminate as much paperwork as possible. One way to accomplish this is through Supplier Certification programs like those mentioned in Chapter One and covered in great detail in *Supplier Certification II: A Handbook for Achieving Excellence Through Continuous Improvement* (PT Publications). With qualified sources, there is no need for inspection, thus eliminating a great deal of paperwork. We have also mentioned bank purchasing card systems as another method of simplifying MRO procurement and reducing paperwork even more. And perhaps the most significant means of reducing or eliminating paperwork is the use of the emerging technology of Electronic Data Interchange (EDI).

EDI is the electronic exchange of business data within a company, between a company and an intermediary network, or directly between two companies. The data is arranged in a structured format so that the sending and receiving computers can "talk" to each other. Most importantly, the structured format allows sending and receiving com-

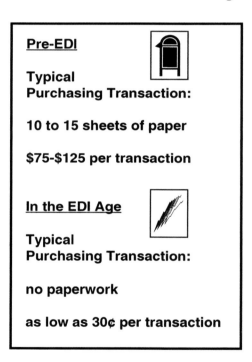

Pre-EDI

**Typical
Purchasing Transaction:**

10 to 15 sheets of paper

$75-$125 per transaction

In the EDI Age

**Typical
Purchasing Transaction:**

no paperwork

as low as 30¢ per transaction

puters to process the data automatically. Prior to EDI, the exchange of routine business information such as sales orders, purchase orders and supplier invoices could create 10 to 15 sheets of paper and cost a company between $100 and $125 per transaction. With EDI, companies have been able to lower this cost to as low as 30 cents with, of course, no creation of paperwork. Imagine the savings that could be generated if a company converted 1,000 purchasing transactions per month from paper to electronic transmissions. What about 10,000 transactions? The savings soon mount up. *EDI Purchasing: The Electronic Gateway to the Future* (PT Publications) will give you even more ideas of what can be accomplished with this new technology.

Blanket Orders and Systems Contracts

Another method of reducing paperwork is the use of blanket order agreements. This is an agreement in which material is released daily / weekly or as required. The objective is to create an environment where the matching of receivers and invoices is eliminated. Closely allied to blanket orders is the systems contracting of MRO supplies. We have found that the following activities and paperwork can be eliminated or reduced:

ELIMINATIONS

1. Purchase orders
2. Acknowledgments
3. Expediting
4. Back orders
5. More than one invoice per month
6. Inventory
7. Sales calls to Purchasing

REDUCTIONS

1. Costs
2. Paperwork
3. Cost of inventory
4. Workload in Purchasing
5. Delays between requisitioner, Purchasing and supplier
6. Phone calls to suppliers
7. Emergencies

For example, let's say that, every month, you buy 2 cases of paper clips in 10 boxes of 1,000. You do this every month, every year without fail. You know some paper clips turn into ear-cleaners, some get sucked up by vacuum cleaners, etc., but 20,000 clips a month serves your purpose. Currently, you send a purchase order every month to your stationery supplier asking for 2 cases. She sends back an acknowledgment; the cases come with an invoice which goes from receiving to Purchasing; the cases are placed in a closet and doled out by an inventory clerk or office manager.

Systems contracting eliminates this inefficiency. You know how many clips you will need over the next year. So, you tell your stationer, "Sue, this year I'm going to buy 240,000 paper clips. But, I want to make a new arrangement with you. I'm sick and tired of going through all the paperwork involved in requisitioning two cases a month. I'll bet you are, too. I know you will always have paper clips in stock. So, from now on, let's have a contract which says I will buy 240,000 paper clips at an agreed upon price and you will deliver them to my company as the storeroom releases them, based on actual requests."

But no supplier, you say, is going to throw a box of 1,000 paper clips on a truck because somebody in your Engineering department ran out of paper clips. Perhaps not. However, it is extremely likely that you do not buy only paper clips from Sue, the stationer. It is also likely that you will be systems contracting for a number of office supplies and, in that case, it is to Sue's benefit and profit to go along with you. But, aren't we just pushing inventory off on the supplier? Not necessarily. As part of your implementation of a systems contract, you have gone through old invoices and determined a usage history for each item. This history, you share with your supplier so that she knows what to expect from your company and, thus, can order appropriately for her own warehouse. This, as you can see, takes coordination and communication. It means that if you see a blip in paper clip consumption appearing in the future, you have to alert her.

And it works. When I worked at Digital Equipment Corporation, we established a relationship with suppliers in which supplies were delivered to each department's secretary as that person placed releases against the contract. Not only did the supplier deliver in small quantities and on time, but to each individual location or secretary. Variations of this also exist where the supplier will consign material to your site and charge you based on consumption.

Lastly, we would like to add a few words about field MRO purchasing. We recommend that branch locations buy supplies from local suppliers. This does not mean, however, that the release and monitoring programs mentioned above are to be ignored. They should be as much a part of the procurement of field MRO supplies as they are at the main offices.

Travel Access of West Palm Beach, FL, goes as far as implementing on-site travel offices for some of their corporate accounts. They pledge to dedicate a full-time consultant to the account whose express purpose is to minimize travel expenses. For clients with domestic and international travel, Travel Access is able to obtain considerable savings from airline fares, hotel rooms and rental cars. In addition, savings can be obtained from minimizing the amount of administrative time that the client company usually invested in travel planning. The use of an MRO supplier who is willing to work with you in finding savings is of paramount importance.

MRO Contracts

The MRO Partnership Agreement spells out the responsibilities of both the customer and the supplier. It is not a purchase order. It works in conjunction with purchasing agreements, blanket orders or system contracts. Instead, it is a mutually developed document which simply provides that the MRO supplier delivers supplies which conform to requirements 100% of the time. Its purpose is to state responsibilities and to create an understanding of the working relationship.

The Contents of a MRO Partnership Agreement

The agreement's purpose is to map out how the customer and the supplier will integrate all of the issues discussed in this chapter. As explained earlier, it will contain a statement of purpose and scope and set objectives:

Terms and Conditions
- Sets quantity levels for supplies or services.
- Defines quality level as zero-defects.
- Controls price fluctuations and conditions for cost/price changes.
- Establishes delivery schedules and windows, as well as shipping terms and packaging specifications.
- Defines terms of payment.
- Establishes responsibilities for corrective action in the event of nonconformance.

In order to have a true partnership, each side must be committed to meeting certain responsibilities. This is the core of any successful agreement. Neither side should feel as though they are being taken advantage of. The following chart illustrates some of the responsibilities of a partner:

RESPONSIBILITIES OF AN MRO SUPPLIER PARTNERSHIP

	Customer	*Supplier*
1.	Clear standards — Quality, Quantity, and Delivery	Evaluate standards/methods
2.	Clear line of communication	Clear line of communication
3.	Notification of organizational changes	Notification of organizational changes
4.	Discussion of potential changes in requirements	Discussion of potential changes in requirements and improvement

5.	Assist supplier in solving quality problems	Notify customer of quality problems
6.	Provide timely feedback and corrective action	Provide timely feedback and corrective action
7.	Provide audit schedule	Notify customer of sourcing or process changes
8.	Share audit results	Close feedback loop
9.	Resolve supplier questions	Inform customer of new processes and /or materials
10.	Commit to continuous improvement program	Commit to continuous improvement program

We invite you to refer to the *Supply Management Toolbox* (PT Publications) for a complete example of a Supplier Partnership Agreement. We also provide a number of other books on contracts as well as ContractWare software for the following categories. ContractWare includes the capability of customizing the sample contracts on-line. The following checklists are for you to use when procuring MRO suppliers and services.

Business Practices

Activity	*Due Date*	*Person Responsible*
Background investigation services		
Electronic payment agreements		
Trading partner agreements		
Hazardous waste agreements		
Hold harmless agreements		
Mutual non-disclosure agreements		
Property disposal services		
Reclamations services		

Capital Equipment

	Due	Person
Activity	*Date*	*Responsible*
Basic capital equipment		
Material handling equipment		
Process systems		
Test equipment		

Contract Manufacturing

	Due	Person
Activity	*Date*	*Responsible*
Repair		
Use of contract letters		
Use of property		
Assembly, fabrication, contract manufacturing		

Distributors

	Due	Person
Activity	*Date*	*Responsible*
Components, peripherals, services		

Facility Services

	Due	Person
Activity	*Date*	*Responsible*
Custodial services		
Elevator		
Heating, ventilation, A/C services		
Landscaping and snow removal		
Roofing services		
Hazardous waste removal		

Human Resources Services

Activity	Due Date	Person Responsible
Consultant services		
Temporary employment		
Pre-employment background checks		
Hold harmless		

Office Supplies

Activity	Due Date	Person Responsible
Copiers and office equipment		
Mailroom services		
External mailrooms		
Furniture, set-up services		
Printing services		
Telecommunication services		

Promotional Services

Activity	Due Date	Person Responsible
Advertising services		
Direct marketing		
Public relations services		

Security Services

Activity	Due Date	Person Responsible
Facility security contracts		
Electronic sweep services		
Audio and video services		

Transportation and Logistics

Activity	Due Date	Person Responsible
Freight		
Customs		
Duty		
Rates		

Travel Services

Activity	Due Date	Person Responsible
Hotels		
Rental cars		
Travel agency services		
Electronic payment agreement		
Non-disclosure agreement		

PLANNING
& SCHEDULING
WITHIN THE
MRO FUNCTION

CHAPTER SIX

    The planning and scheduling of MRO procurement relies upon the coordination of maintenance and inventory systems as well as the utilization of MRP (Material Requirements Planning) tools. This coordination oversees requisitions and purchase orders and bills of material. MRP is a computerized system in which bills of material are exploded and consolidated to come up with a precise, real-time picture of MRO needs. Its use as a methodology for determining dependent demand, such as preventive maintenance tasks, is becoming more prevalent. This information is passed on to a buyer/ planner who then purchases the required material from suppliers. In the future, we would like to see this process collapse even further, so that operators, supervisors and receiving personnel would release the information, based on 100% accurate bills of material, directly to the supplier. This would free Purchasing to be responsible for negotiating terms and conditions and long-term agreements.

Bills of Material

Bills of material accurately list the items used in producing a finished good, scheduling parts usage for preventive maintenance, or providing a service. Purchasing must insist on a 100% accurate bill of materials. Incorrect bills lead to faulty planning and poor execution. For example, if a bill lists a component not used, either inventory will grow or someone must intervene and cancel an order for that component. If that person forgets or goes on vacation, unnecessary inventory will be procured and stored. Conversely, if a bill does not list a required component, either the required material will be missing or a "catch-up shortage" environment will be created. In either example, it is far easier to maintain an accurate bill of material which negates the need for special handling.

Inventory Control and Record Accuracy

When it comes to inventory, record accuracy is an issue requiring attention. Whether your storerooms are closed, open or limited has an effect on planning. However, training and educating employees in record accuracy is the primary focus. Storeroom employees must know procedures which ensure accuracy and require follow-up audits. Cycle counting and especially control group counting should be focused on determining the root cause of errors, not just correcting balances. We should also mention quality's role with relationship to inventory. The inventory record compiled by an MRP system assumes all inventory is good. Some method of quality control should be evaluated and implemented so that available inventory is, in fact, free of defects. Again, supplier certification is a key component of this.

We have been discussing the ingredients — inventory, bills of material, etc. — used in the MRO recipe. These ingredients are mixed in the computer and out comes a material plan, using the following series of steps:

1. Explode the bills of material from the preventive maintenance schedule to determine the gross requirement for MRO components.

2. Net the on-hand inventory balance against the gross requirement.

3. Look for any open orders which can be rescheduled to meet demand.

4. Recommend an order quantity using lot size, due date and lead time information.

The power of this system rests in the computer's ability to manipulate massive amounts of data in a quick and accurate manner. This manipulation of data determines what material is needed and when it should be purchased. Most systems today also allow for the allocation of inventory which exists in the storeroom, but which may be allotted for near-term requirements. In short, MRP allows companies to control a process which is subject to frequent changes in orders, inventory records and bills of material.

Purchasing

Purchasing has the responsibility of contracting with suppliers for the purchase of MRO materials, goods and services to meet the requirements of the facility. In essence, MRP substitutes accurate information for inventory. And this information works in two ways. One, it allows you to see what is going on inside your plant. You can substitute advance knowledge for overstocked storage areas and personal stockpiles. Why? Because you know what we need and when. The second way information helps is by allowing you to alert suppliers as to what you will need and when. Planning has to extend beyond the bounds of the facility. In this way, safety stocks can be eliminated.

Preventive Maintenance

Companies should also be gathering and reviewing data at regular intervals in order to determine the mean time between failures. This review will allow companies to make more informed decisions. They will be able to accurately determine the life of a belt, a bearing or a gear by looking at the frequency of replacement in the past. Then, they can start replacing equipment parts during down time or during scheduled maintenance time. In other words, fix the equipment just before it deteriorates or breaks down. World Class organizations typically go beyond preventive maintenance and include condition-based monitoring and zero breakdown in their programs. These methods yield a wealth of information that can further reduce failure rates.

Once the failure rate is determined, you should start working with your production schedule people to get the necessary time to repair a machine in order to perform preventive maintenance. It should be emphasized that if maintenance schedule attainment is not measured and enforced with the same degree of discipline as production, then zero-breakdown maintenance will not work.

Look for opportunities to utilize the supplier's expertise in reducing breakdowns. Techniques such as condition-based monitoring are a good example of value-added activity by a supplier. Often, however, management is not concerned enough with preventive maintenance. Instead of finding ways to prevent outbreaks of problems, they spend a majority of their time putting out the fires caused by maintenance problems. Management should be alerted to the benefits of preventive maintenance. We have found that companies can achieve the following results from a preventive maintenance program:

- **Increased machine availability.**
- **Reduced spare parts inventory.**
- **Improved planning and execution of maintenance work orders.**
- **More efficient planning for turnarounds and shutdowns.**
- **Faster response to emergency work.**
- **Higher return on investments.**
- **Smoother maintenance scheduling.**
- **Lower total cost.**
- **Less downtime.**
- **Increased equipment life.**
- **Improved quality.**

As for emergency repairs, we believe that this is a critical area to measure in order to see how well a preventive maintenance program is working. Keep in mind, however, that in the short and intermediate term not all emergencies can be eliminated. It is possible to prevent 80% of them. When this is the case, it is possible to respond more quickly and efficiently to the emergencies which occur in the remaining 20% of the time because everything is not a "red-hot" emergency.

When establishing preventive maintenance, make certain that you include the operators of the machinery as the first line of defense. It is very easy for an operator to check fluid levels, for example, of oil, water or hydraulic fluid. We recommend providing your operators with an easy-to-follow checklist which keeps words to a minimum and relies on well-known symbols. For example, put a picture of a dipstick on the form to remind an operator to check the oil level. If you put an acetate sheet over this form, the operator merely has to "x" the picture to indicate that it has been done.

PREVENTIVE MAINTENANCE CHECKLIST					
	Mon	Tues	Wed	Thurs	Fri
Water		✓		✓	
Oil		✓	✓		✓
Hydraulic			✓	✓	

Quick Release Programs

Quick release programs are a collection of techniques mentioned in this chapter and earlier chapters. They should be consolidated into one strategy with cycle time reduction and quality products and services as the focus. Early Supplier Involvement (ESI) in the development of delivery systems for products and services is becoming more widespread. Early involvement allows purchasing to work with suppliers in shortening lead times, eliminating paperwork and lowering costs.

MANAGING THE COMMUNICATIONS

CHAPTER SEVEN

There are many more options available today for managing communications about MRO procurement. Telephones, beepers and fax machines are being joined by the technology of EDI and the global advent of the Internet. Whatever the technology, however, communication comes down to building long-term partnerships with strategic suppliers. The benefits of a win/win partnership are present throughout an organization, but let's concentrate here on the reduction in paperwork. Conventional practices (which are still used all too often) dictate that purchasing personnel stay in their offices, send out detailed RFQs and then select the supplier with the best price. Contracts are hammered out in which both parties argue about variances. Today, purchasing personnel go out and visit suppliers with a set of supply performance specifications. The supplier and customer work together to meet these specifications. The difference this means in the amount of paperwork is shown in Figure 7-1.

Paperwork Reduction

From:	To:
• Purchase order	• Supplier schedule
• P.O. amendment	— Schedule sharing
• Move tag	— EDI
• Bill of lading	• Shipment authorization
• Invoice	cards
• Receiving report	• Systems contracting
• Packing slip	
• Check	

Figure 7-1.

Based on our experience at Pro-Tech, we have developed a list of the key elements of a win/win partnership between a customer and supplier. The following listing comes from our Supplier Cooperation Agreement in Chapter 13 of the *Supply Management Toolbox* (PT Publications):

> **Declaration of Intent** — Commitment expressed by company and supplier to the philosophy of total customer satisfaction.

Days	Flexibility cancel/change	
0 - 30	XX%	(20 - 25)
31 - 60	XX%	(50)
61 - 90	XX%	(100)
91+	XX%	(100)

> **Just-In-Time Purchasing** — Visibility of company's long-term commodity requirements through use of Flexibility Window.

Early Supplier Involvement in Design — Formal program to gather their input into the design for more flexibility.

Cooperation Team — Opening of a line of communication between the company and the supplier in order to initiate and drive continuous improvement activities.

Cooperation Mutual Disclosure — The company and its suppliers will openly discuss requirements of end customer, procurement of materials, design, delivery times and costs.

Performance Measurement — Measurement of continuous improvement will be monitored to satisfy company's delivery, quality, cost reduction and service requirements.

Scope of Technical Cooperation — Company and suppliers will divulge relevant technology to each other.

Delivery Cycle Time Reduction — Supplier will take initiative to decrease the cycle time on parts/process delivery.

Packing, Return Packaging — Supplier will work with company to develop environmentally compatible, returnable packaging.

Quality Systems Requirements — The supplier will work with company to attain world class quality and reliability through superior design, process controls and continuous process improvements.

Supplier Survey Results — The supplier will work toward developing a world class level of six sigma quality.

Meetings — Meetings shall be held regularly to review cost reduction and continuous improvement.

Preferred Supplier — Realization of benefits resulting from Preferred Supplier status.

Patents and Other Rights — Rights to ideas, inventions, know-how emanating from the parties' cooperation shall remain with the originator.

Training and Education Effectiveness — Content and usefulness of customer's formal supplier training programs.

Confidentiality — All information shared by the company and the supplier shall be treated in confidence.

It is clear that suppliers are looking for a great deal in a supplier partnership and that is good for the customer. If all of the criteria listed above were put into effect, the customer would benefit as much as the supplier. Remember: It's a *partnership*, so both sides should win.

The Benefits of Supplier Partnerships

What exactly are the benefits of a supplier partnership between you and an MRO supplier? It is difficult to speak about benefits without also discussing the responsibilities of both parties. There are some responsibilities and benefits which are particular to the supplier or customer and some which are shared by both. Whatever the particular blend, the mutual benefits are listed here:

• **Trust and Loyalty** — the bedrock upon which the partnership stands.

- **Long-Term Marriage** — as long as both partners work at the relationship, everybody wins.

- **Win/Win Relationship** — cost savings are shared by both partners.

- **Mutually Acceptable Specifications** — the supplier is involved early in the development process.

- **Financial Incentives/Penalties** — the success of one partner guarantees the success of the other.

- **Improved Profitability** — embracing new paradigms lead to mutual rewards.

The reciprocal relationship of both benefits and responsibilites is what cements the bond between the two parties to the Supply Management agreement. Now, the question remains as to how to attain the relationship with suppliers which has been outlined so far.

Designing an Organizational Survey

Part of the process of fostering win/win partnerships is accomplished through surveys which measure the strengths, weaknesses and needs of an organization. Besides identifying areas of opportunity for improving conditions, products or processes, surveys can also help to locate attitudinal problems and suggest ways to encourage people to take part in teams. Done correctly, a survey will cement the long-term MRO supply relationship.

Collecting meaningful and accurate data is the result of careful planning and testing. The first step in gaining feedback about internal customer satisfaction is to define your goals. Describe the desired outcome of the survey. What kind of data will be obtained by this survey? In order to pinpoint what is to be accomplished by a survey, begin by establishing priorities. The checklist below will help you to prioritize needs:

Goals of an Organizational Survey

Number the following items from 1 to 10 in order of priority (10 being that item on which you would place the highest priority need).

_____ Define our organization's strengths and weaknesses.

_____ Evaluate our internal communication effectiveness.

_____ Realize how our people view their ability to work productively.

_____ Learn what motivates our people to achieve.

_____ Identify more effective ways of employing our resources.

_____ Become more responsive to our customer needs.

_____ Become more responsive to the needs of our people.

_____ Encourage our people to contribute ideas for improvement.

_____ Develop leadership skills at all levels.

_____ Improve our organization's ability to perform.

Surveys and Feedback

All well-designed organizational surveys give prompt feedback to the participants in the survey. Feedback shows that you are serious about the survey and, more importantly, that you are serious about a win/win partnership. Results of the survey can be distributed through short memos, reports, newsletters, voluntary discussion sessions and even bulletin boards. Survey results can also work to bring groups together for the first time as they talk about what the results mean and what should be done. In a certain sense, feedback is the means for gaining grassroots activism. The purpose of surveys and feedback is to get people talking to each other so they will be motivated to change what needs improvement.

Gaining Support and "Buy-In"

For any win/win partnership to be successful, it will need the full support of the people who are participating. Above all, people must understand that this process is a continuous striving for improvement and not just a one-time event. Equally as important is the necessity of allowing people to "buy in" to the process and not to force them into it. JAL, Japan Airlines, accomplishes this with a concept called *kizuki* which are elite corps of engineers who are assigned to their own 747s. They then become obsessed with performance. When a team "owns" what it is doing, the level of excellence increases dramatically. Assigning supplier employees to extended teams is an example of how this principle applies.

Management can also help the process of "buying in" by demonstrating it themselves. Recently a company initiated a people involvement/empowerment process and, to show their commitment, management took pay cuts up to 15 percent. Management can also obtain support by informing its people about the market and competition the company is up against. The key here is to treat suppliers as important components who have the need to know how to do their job better. Let your MRO suppliers know why it is important to reduce costs, to modernize, to change from the old ways of doing business to the new ways. The best way to institute the change process is to show that you believe in it.

Strategy for Change

As with most plans of action, the strategy for implementing a win/win partnership begins with realizing and defining the need for change. Once the need is established, then you can begin determining and reviewing competitive issues. Management should not suppress any of the issues which surround the effects of change. Being competitive in a world class marketplace means achieving a level of excellence in which strategy shapes and is, in turn, shaped by your corporate culture. You want to create a culture in which desirable traits are developed with careful attention to the needs of the organization as well as the needs of people. Culture and strategy unite in the common purpose of communicating how win/win partnerships are managed.

Our advice for companies wishing to build a World Class model of MRO procurement is to begin with only "A" suppliers from a Pareto ranking of MRO suppliers in order to develop a pilot program. We also strongly advocate documenting and communicating the results of your efforts in order to build ownership in the process. The key to implementation is to involve the whole company, and the first stage in the process is training and education. This is followed by the establishment of a steering committee and then the establishment of teams which will attack and solve problems. Lastly, measurements must be put in place in order to compare today's status with established benchmarks and objectives.

Competency Model

Training and education for suppliers is extremely important in meeting objectives today and tomorrow. The goal is to provide a positive atmosphere which will stimulate suppliers to discuss theory, practices and alternatives. Training should be based on supplier competency and focused on creating greater cross-functional awareness.

The first priority in planning a training and education program for MRO suppliers and buyers is to assess all their requirements. We have developed a competency model (Figure 8-1) which will assist you in defining where your suppliers are proficient or deficient. The numbers indicate the necessary levels of expertise for each function. By comparing the levels of expertise within the supplier's company to the desired levels in the chart, you can determine short-term and long-term objectives required for education and training.

Education and Training

Each supplier needs to provide opportunities for education and training. Education encourages cross-fertilization of ideas and must provide the following:

- **A clear understanding of MRO procurement objectives.**
- **A positive climate to express ideas without fear.**
- **An environment for active participation.**
- **A process for strategic decision-making about suppliers.**
- **Ability to achieve problem resolution.**
- **System to measure success.**

Competency Model for Determining Knowledge and Skill Requirements By Function

COMPETENCY AREAS	FUNCTIONS							
	Maintenance	Finance	Sales	Production	Quality	Purchasing	Planning	Traffic
Inventory Mgmt.	3	3	3	3	3	3	3	3
Set-up Reduction	1	2	1	3	3	3	3	1
Supplier Cert.	2	1	2	3	3	3	3	3
SPC/TQC	2	1	1	3	3	3	3	2
Preventive Maint.	3	1	1	3	1	1	2	1
Value Analysis	1	1	1	3	3	3	3	2
EDI	2	3	3	3	3	3	3	3
Planning	2	3	2	3	2	3	3	3

1. indicates a familiarity with subject
2. requires a working knowledge of field
3. requires expertise in area

Figure 8-1.

Direction

A company must establish a direction in order to manage the implementation of world class programs. The aim is to organize a commodity and process around clearly stated aims and goals that can be handled by less senior buyers. The general rule is that a team should have eight to ten members and that for every salaried or management person, there should be an hourly laborer. However, for MRO, the number can be two to three because of the value of the commodities being purchased. That number will get the job done. Teams should include the supplier, the internal customer and the buyer.

Selecting a Team to Develop the Results

When selecting the people who will serve on your team, we believe that every person who works for your organization is a potential candidate and source of valuable information. We further emphasize time and time again that it is not necessary for all team members to have an MRO purchasing background. In fact, it is sometimes detrimental for a team to have a traditional mindset. A new perspective, what we call a "different set of eyes," is often very helpful to a team.

We like a team to be multifunctional and multilevel. Every effort should be made to select representatives from each of the organizational levels that is required as shown in Figure 8-2. After the team members have been selected, your company's next step is to train them to function as a team. It is extremely important that a team develops a sense of cooperation and ownership early in the process in order to make the most of their time together.

Measurements

One of the hardest tasks facing a company is establishing meaningful MRO measurements. Take a look at your current measurements. How many of your current measurements complement and interface with each other? You must be sure that all measurements are interrelated. The key is to establish a benchmark today with goals and objectives which must be met. Once a baseline is established, you should measure and monitor your progress toward the goal. Perhaps most importantly, measurements are useful as a dynamic management tool which establishes a results orientation in the workplace. We

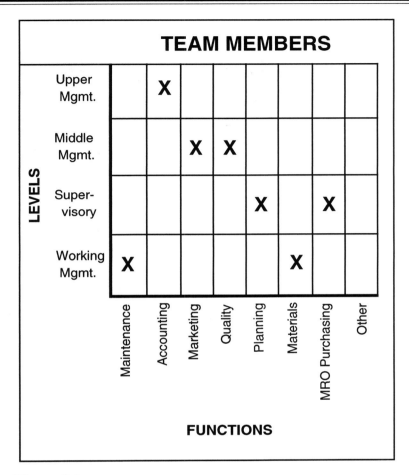

Figure 8-2.

have included Figure 8-3 to help you on the path to obtaining these desired results.

Continuous Improvement: The Goal of Measurement

When we look at continuous improvement, it rests on the measurement of only four critical performance areas. Every organization, company, department or function, whether they produce products or

What steps should be employed in developing and implementing a successful Purchasing Performance Measurement Program for MRO supplies?

Define Criteria and Responsibility

What will be measured? _____

How? _____

Reporting vehicle? _____

What should the responsible employee/function do? _____

Establish Goals and Objectives

What are we trying to accomplish? _____

Why? _____

Benefits? _____

How will you attain them? _____

How will we know when we get there? _____

Implement Benchmarking

What are best-in-class performance levels? _____

Gap identification? _____

Cycle time reporting? _____

Who will provide data? _____

Which companies can contribute? _____

Where will you obtain consulting assistance? _____

Measure and Monitor Performance

Reporting cycles must be established. Who will monitor: _____

Progress? _____

Performance? _____

Timetables? _____

Review Results and Required Actions

What levels are involved? _____

Top management? _____

What are the intermediate milestones? _____

Determine Corrective Action Required

Policy (s)? _____

Procedural? _____

Ongoing development? _____

Who is responsible? _____

Figure 8-3.

provide services, has two external performance objectives. They are meeting or exceeding customer requirements 100% of the time and 100% on-time delivery of products or services to the customer, whether that is the end user or the next station on the production line. Every organization, company, department or function, whether they produce products or provide services, also has two internal performance objectives. They are reducing the cycle time it takes to produce or provide the product or service and reducing or eliminating all nonvalue-added activities from the cycle.

Whatever measurements you devise to help your organization efficiently control its supply base, they must adhere to this rule of continuous improvement. Such measurements will also indicate where more efforts are indicated and serve as an objective and visible motivational prod to further action. You can turn your procurement of MRO supplies and services into a world class operation.

Resources

Additional Purchasing Resources from PT Publications, Inc.

P.O. Box 310266
Miami, FL 33231
1-800-547-426

THE PURCHASING ENCYCLOPEDIA

Just-In-Time Purchasing: In Pursuit of Excellence $29.95
      Peter L. Grieco, Jr., Michael W. Gozzo and Jerry W. Claunch

---

Glossary of Key Purchasing Terms, Acronyms, and Formulas PT Publications	$14.95
Supplier Certification II: A Handbook for *Achieving Excellence through Continuous Improvement* Peter L. Grieco, Jr.	$49.95
EDI Purchasing: The Eletronic Gateway to the Future Steven Marks	$14.95
World Class: Measuring Its Achievement Peter L. Grieco, Jr.	$39.95
Purchasing Performance Measurements: A Roadmap For Excellence Mel Pilachowski	$12.95
The World Of Negotiations: Never Being a Loser Peter L. Grieco, Jr. and Paul G. Hine	$39.95
How To Conduct Supplier Surveys and Audits Janet L. Przirembel	$14.95
Supply Management Toolbox: How to Manage Your Suppliers Peter L. Grieco, Jr.	$26.95
Purchasing Capital Equipment Thomas E. Petroski	$14.95
Power Purchasing: Supply Management in the 21st Century Peter L. Grieco, Jr. and Carl R. Cooper	$39.95
Global Sourcing Lee Krotseng	$14.95
Purchasing Ethics Peter L. Grieco, Jr.	$14.95
Purchasing Contract Law, UCC, and Patents Mark Grieco	$14.95
EDI Purchasing: The Electronic Gateway to the Future Steven Marks	$14.95
Site Smart Purchasing Craig A. Melby and Jane Utzman	$14.95
MRO Purchasing Peter L. Grieco, Jr.	$14.95
*The Complete Guide to Contracts Management For **Facilities Services*** John P. Mahoney and Linda S. Keckler	$18.95
*The Complete Guide to Contracts Management For **Components*** John P. Mahoney and Linda S. Keckler	$23.95
*The Complete Guide to Contracts Management For **Promotional Services*** William F. Badenhoff and John P. Mahoney	$18.95
*The Complete Guide to Contracts Management For **Business Practices*** William F. Badenhoff and John P. Mahoney	$23.95
*The Complete Guide to Contracts Management For **Office Services*** John P. Mahoney and William F. Badenhoff	$16.95

*The Complete Guide to Contracts Management For **Peripherals*** $23.95
John P. Mahoney and William F. Badenhoff
*The Complete Guide to Contracts Management For **Capital Equipment*** $14.95
John P. Mahoney and William F. Badenhoff
The Complete Guide to Contracts Management $16.95
*For **Human Resources Services***
John P. Mahoney and Linda S. Keckler
*The Complete Guide to Contracts Management For **Security Services*** $16.95
William F. Badenhoff and John P. Mahoney
*The Complete Guide to Contracts Management For **Contract Manufacturing*** $23.95
John P. Mahoney and William F. Badenhoff
*The Complete Guide to Contracts Management For **Distributors*** $18.95
John P. Mahoney and William F. Badenhoff
The Complete Guide to Contracts Management For $18.95
Transportation and Logistics Services Volume 1
John P. Mahoney and Linda S. Keckler
The Complete Guide to Contracts Management For $18.95
Transportation and Logistics Services Volume 2
John P. Mahoney and Linda S. Keckler
*The Complete Guide to Contracts Management For **Travel Services*** $16.95
John P. Mahoney and Linda S. Keckler

PURCHASING VIDEO EDUCATION SERIES

Supplier Certification The Path to Excellence
Tape 1: *Why Supplier Certification?* $395.00
Tape 2: *Quality at the Supplier* $395.00
Tape 3: *How to Select a Supplier* $395.00
Tape 4: *Supplier Surveys and Audits* $395.00
Tape 5: *Supplier Quality Agreements* $395.00
Tape 6: *Supplier Ratings* $395.00
Tape 7: *Phases of Supplier Certification* $395.00
Tape 8: *Implementing a Supplier Certification Program* $395.00
Tape 9: *Evaluating Your Supplier Certification Program* $395.00

Complete Nine Tape Series $1,995.00

PURCHASING AUDIO TAPES

The World of Negotiations: How to Win Every Time $39.95

RESOURCES

PURCHASING SOFTWARE

Supplier Survey and Audit Forms Developed by Professionals For Technology, Inc.	$395.00

ContractWare™
Developed by The Leadership Companies, Inc.

Business Practices	$599.00
Capital Equipment	$599.00
Components	$599.00
Peripherals	$599.00
Contract Manufacturing	$599.00
Distributors	$599.00
Facilities Management	$599.00
Human Resources	$599.00
Office Services	$599.00
Promotional Services	$599.00
Security Services	$599.00
Transportation and Logistics	$599.00
Travel Services	$599.00
Site License (unlimited users per site)	Call
Corporate License (unlimited users, unlimited sites)	Call
Administrative Library Database (requires site of corporate license)	Call

CyberBase™
Client Server Software containing all 14 contract families
Developed by the Leadership Companies, Inc.

Individual Server Licenses	Call
Corporate License (unlimited servers, unlimited users)	Call
Additional Installations	Call

ADDITIONAL PROFESSIONAL TEXTBOOKS

Failure Modes and Effects Analysis: Predicting *and Preventing Problems Before They Occur* Paul Palady	$39.95
Made In America: The Total Business Concept Peter L. Grieco, Jr. and Michael W. Gozzo	$29.95
Reengineering Through Cycle Time Management Wayne L. Douchkoff and Thomas E. Petroski	$39.95

Behind Bars: Bar Coding Principles and Applications $39.95
    Peter L. Grieco, Jr., Michael W. Gozzo and C.J. (Chip) Long
People Empowerment: Achieving Success from Involvement $39.95
    Michael W. Gozzo and Wayne L. Douchkoff
Activity Based Costing: The Key to World Class Performance $18.00
    Peter L. Grieco, Jr. and Mel Pilachowski

Index

A
ABB (Asea Brown Boveri) 21
Administration 39-40
Avnet-EMG 55

B
Baldrige award 16
Bar coding 56
Baselines 86
Benchmarking 17-18, 88

INDEX

S

Sector sourcing 24-25

Security services 67

Selecting distributors 30-31

Selecting OEMs 30-31

Service management 36

Strategies 3, 82

Statistical Process Control (SPC) 28

Storage management 41-42

Supplier cooperation agreement 76-78

Supplier partnerships 64-65

Supplier reduction 6

Supplier selection 4, 7-8

Supplier selection criteria 7

Supplier stocking 6

Supply chain 2

Supply management 40-41

Survey and audit form

  MRO distributor 38-44

  MRO suppliers 33-37

Surveys and audits 10

Systems contracts 61-63

T

Teambuilding 85-86

Total cost approach 14

Transportation and logistics 68

Travel Access 63

Travel services 68

W

Warehouses 55-56